Kolme | Tre –
Three Poets from Finland

Ralf Andtbacka, Marko Hautala
and Carita Nyström

smith|doorstop

Published 2018 by
Smith|Doorstop Books
The Poetry Business
Campo House,
54 Campo Lane,
Sheffield S1 2EG
www.poetrybusiness.co.uk

Copyright © Ralf Andtbacka, Marko Hautala and Carita Nyström 2018
All Rights Reserved

978-1-912196-06-7

Designed and typeset by Utter
Printed by Biddles

Smith|Doorstop books are a member of Inpress:
www.inpressbooks.co.uk. Distributed by NBN International, Airport Business Centre, 10 Thornbury Road Plymouth PL6 7PP.

The Poetry Business gratefully acknowledges the support
of Arts Council England.

Contents

Ralf Andtbacka   7

8	There Was Someone
9	Apples and Oranges
10	Autumn Song
11	Tout le monde est triste
12	Light Elegy
13	Heart's Cattle
14	Last Days in the Rainy Kingdom
15	Perhaps You Can't Die
16	Little Hammer
17	Come Over Here and Tell It to My Knife
17	Kom hit och säg det till min kniv
18	Blue Stone and Book
19	In the Book Mines

Marko Hautala   21

22	The Birth of Frost
23	It Lived
24	Sense
25	Green
26	Nonsense
27	The Dog
28	A Poem
30	A Song
31	Idio(t)s

Carita Nyström   33

34   The Greenhouse in Winter
35   A Travelling Companion
36   The Wolf's Loop
37   White Whales in the White Sea
38   Solovetskij
39   Lethe's River
40   Loss
41   The Chaffinch in the Graveyard
42   Give Grief Your Time
43   Ge din tid åt sorgen
44   Orrmoan – The Devil's Field
45   In The Archipelago
46   The Labyrinth
47   Moment

In our archipelago you find surprisingly many single-path stone-labyrinths. In Finnish they have many names, but in Finland-Swedish mostly 'jungfrudans' (maiden's dance) is used. The labyrinth figure, however, is known over the whole world.

Troy-town (English), Caerdroia (Welsh), Trojenborg (Swedish/Finnish), Babylon (Russia), chemins de Jerusalem (French), Pietarinleikki (Finnish folk interpretation), Wunderbergs (Germany), Völundarhus (Iceland)

From *The Fascinating and mysterious stone-labyrinths,* Vesa Heinonen, trans. Carita Nyström

Ralf Andtbacka

'In a recent interview, the American poet and literary theorist Charles Bernstein said that you must learn to accept that you're a poet the way you learn to accept some unpleasant aspect of yourself. This is mystifying, I immediately thought, but his typically pointed remark nonetheless struck a chord. I stick with poetry because I see no other option. For me, poetry is what's left.

Time passes. I write, I fail, I try again. Writing is mostly a record of failure – on a personal, artistic, and communicative level. Language is unstable. It slips away, dissolves, transmutes. It always does something different than what was hoped for. As I get older, I realise how foolish and pretentious it would be to ask for anything else.

The poems in this short anthology cover a period of almost thirty years. They don't give a full picture of my work, a fair share of my writing is conceptual and not very easy to translate or present in snatches, but they do exemplify a tone and perspective I keep returning to.'

– Vaasa/Vasa, March 2018

There Was Someone

there was someone who felt the skull beneath the skin
someone who felt the word in his mouth

who kept on walking feeling nothing
but his foot and gait   night fell

where he lay on eggs
those that hatched were enough

for a decent breakfast
he survived I suppose

unless cancer got him
. . .

Apples and Oranges

A man leaves home,
the place where he was lit out of nothingness
like a small beacon on the seaboard.
He travels the world
to places he had never known about,
exotic and beautiful places,
where strangers look at him
the way you look at strangers.
By and by, places, glances
stick to his skin like spores,
his skin is transformed
into a milky galaxy of corrosive spores
sinking calmly inside him
at the same velocity as time,
down to the place where
the nothingness out of which he was born
now rests.

. . .

Autumn Song

She loved you, you write. Her moods
like the weather, and the days grew shorter,
until only the bus journey home was left
                             Kisses goodbye
September drained of meaning, October tidies the crowns of trees
as the caretaker turns off the lights in freshly waxed corridors

Always a little forgetfulness hibernates in us
until next summer bursts loose   By then she was gone
Initials blacken in the bark, swallows swoop even closer

                          And the world gives way
Our wishes come true through an inversion
and one day we realize that nothing weighs less
than our bodies   It's like seeing oneself naked in a mirror
for the first time   This piece of knowledge we carry with us
to innumerable dates and experience a peculiar sense of lightness
as though the last dance (drunkenness, cock stiffening
against her belly) never should end any other way
. . .

Tout le monde est triste

One drowsy day in August we rowed out on the bay,
first through the canal and then along the dredged channel.
There is a small island out there, covered with birches, alders,
and some resin-dripping conifers, not a spectacular place,
but still a piece of land separated from land.
So we rowed there, jumped out of the boat, dragged it ashore.
It took us fifteen minutes to walk around the island,
without seeing anything out of the ordinary:
an oil can, some rotten boards, smashed bottles, uprooted trees.
Sedge-grass and reeds. Squawking birds. And then
we left. Back out on the water my friend said:
        In autumn the old bull elk swims there
                and waits until the hunting-season is over.
He was lying, of course. In silence
we listened to the dip of the oars, both of us thinking
about elks swimming, the jerky movement,
    heads cleaving
        the glistening surface.

. . .

Light Elegy

And that's why the river must make its way to the sea,
never the other way around

Some boulders are pushed aside,
others tumble down to the river bed, where the miracle happens once again

At night, too, when a barge cleaves the muddy surface,
believing it belongs to a chastened channel,

perhaps as part of a clandestine network
oxygenating the land;

the place we've learned to love,
at times thanks to the carrot, at times

thanks to the stick
But there must always be something else,

buildings with open doors, with sliding doors
front and back, so that you can look

through them, just like you look through people
you don't have anything to offer

or paper-thin insects in August, greenish
against a blue, blue August sky
...

Heart's Cattle

Stop by the gate, open
the gate. The gate is already
open. For heart's cattle.
Emaciated creatures, starving.
The pen is full of grass.
Thirsty creatures, reeling.
Now a well springs
from their animal hearts.

. . .

Last Days in the Rainy Kingdom
For Peter Didsbury

All the forests are drenched
the roads muddy and no longer
passable. The brooks are foaming,
the mere dark and heavy.
Oh, I don't want this rain to stop,
one of the king's scribes notes,
I wish our dreams
were different from our aching hearts.
I only wish there was no time
to mourn this sweet but decaying kingdom.
Already his face blurred
as the writing on the softened scroll.
And the days passed by,
               and the clouds passed by,
as though the rain had never stopped.
. . .

Perhaps You Can't Die

in a dream,
sitting behind drawn curtains.
All the clocks have stopped.

Only time is keeping time.

We have lived.
We have lived and learned.
We have lived and learned and eaten well.

Our shadows still linger.
. . .

Little Hammer

Today the maple outside the factory gate
is prayer, speech impediment, holy fire.

I have a Hello Kitty band-aid slapped on the bridge
of my nose. My jacket bleeds feathers.

Little hammer ringing against the anvil.
My two irises are knots of holy fire.

Now the Queen of Greasy Hair emerges,
wearing the same drab coat she always wears.

The pavement smoulders where she treads.
. . .

Come Over Here and Tell It to My Knife

slicing bread is like:
holding a new-born baby:
you must be careful:
but resolute too:
let your knife do the slicing:
not your hand:
the only thing your hand does:
is move back and forth:
back and forth.
. . .

Kom hit och säg det till min kniv

att skära bröd är som:
att hålla i ett nyfött barn:
man måste vara försiktig:
men bestämd:
skär med kniven:
inte med handen:
allt din hand ska göra är:
dra fram och tillbaka:
fram och tillbaka.
. . .

Blue Stone and Book

the sky's so big and the cloud's so small:
if you really want to catch a fish: you'll have
to die with the fish: soon it'll be over: it'll be over –
and soon: blue stone and book: taking hold
in the dark: like tiny apertures: or these three phrases
keeping track of us: one mouth and a pair of eyes:
light a candle to look at the woods: a neighbour
with no neighbours is not a pretty sight:
a forest with no trees is not a pretty sight:
but a mouth without a smile:

is like a leaf.
. . .

In the Book Mines

Caught inside a summer flu and a series of dreams.
You can't clear your lungs of phlegm any more.
You cough, you hawk, but nothing helps.
At some point you drift into restless sleep.

You're working in the book mines.
You scratch and pick away.
Book dust claiming still more victims.

You're working in the book graveyard,
digging new graves in the print soil,
cutting pages open with a spade.

You're a farmhand at the book farm.
You blacken and dung the land.
Sweet Jesus, how you dung the land.

. . .

Marko Hautala

'After writing eight novels and not a single poem in over ten years, my work on this anthology involved a lot of uncertainty. In a novel you can, with a little bit of practice, make anything appear natural or inevitable. Poetry is a different game altogether.

To me the main challenge in writing poems is finding a voice that can speak calmly and clearly about things that are a complete mess. If you identify too much with the mess itself, the poem just imitates the chaos around you. If you try to force the mess into a pretty dress and tell it to play an old accordion, it looks stupid.

In prose you have age-old structures, character arcs and plot devices to help maintain the right balance. In poetry you just have to write and rewrite until a voice says *now, there*.'

– Vaasa/Vasa, March 2018

The Birth of Frost

I learned a cold fact when I was five, walking on a field with my dad.
There will be frost tonight, he said. The stars are bright.
Bright stars make the frost? I asked.
No, he said. When the frost is coming, the stars are bright.
So frost makes stars bright? I asked.
He stopped, lit a cigarette. Its end a tiny, weak sun against the dark.
We'll be cold, he said. You'll see.

It Lived

In 1551 an unknown creature washed ashore in Norway.
The locals called it Monk Fish because what they thought was the front part
Looked like the shaved head of a monk.
Under it was something like a cape
Fins instead of arms
Broad tail at the bottom –
But all this with a 'coarse and rude outline'
Which means that the villagers and fishermen had no idea
What had entered their world.

So the story begins and ends with:
In 1551 an unknown creature washed ashore in Norway.
And a brief epilogue:
It lived for three days and did not produce a sound
except for some deep sighs, indicating distress and sorrow.

Sense

A mystery: when scientists first started capturing ceratioid anglerfish,
They noticed that all the specimens were female.
And they all had several parasites attached to them.
How could they survive? And where were the males?
Eventually they found that the parasites
Were in reality male ceratioid anglerfish.
That they bite into the female's skin
And release an enzyme that melds them together
Until they have one shared blood circulation.

When the female dies
The male lives on for a while.
A pointless existence in absolute darkness.
In a pressure fifteen thousand times the air pressure.
Yet. Somehow. It has always made sense.

Green

The last time I saw her.
She didn't know where or who.
Several machines with tubes.
Like in an experiment.
I was expecting more white.
Fearing its glow in advance.
But the curtains were green.
Like grass.
Waving.
Not knowing.
Where or who.

Nonsense

In ancient Egyptian tombs the main vault could be as deep
As thirteen hundred feet underground. Hundreds of people
Would work to build it, most of them not slaves but paid labour:
Engineers, diggers, caterers, priests, embalmers, artists, poets.
The best eyes the best hands the best minds of a civilisation
Focused on not food and war but

The dead
The afterlife,
No surplus,
No proof,
Just plain nonsense.

And yet the economy thrived more or less
For four thousand years and some.
In any case, longer than ours. By far.

In the tomb of Ramses the Third, in the main vault thirteen
                              hundred feet down,
One more passageway descended even deeper underground
Into nothing. There was no additional vault. No purpose.
It was a passage into the nonsense
That somehow made it all work.

The Dog

I never saw my grandfather cry.
Even on the way to a funeral he was joking –
About the deceased
And my grandmother, and my dad who was driving.

Later, at his own funeral
A hunting dog appeared out of nowhere
And walked beside the procession barking.

Then they realised the coffin wouldn't fit into the grave.
A frozen moment. Confusion. Horror.
The priest didn't know what to say.
My grandmother had always been careful
Not to invite gossip. And now this.
In a small town the story would outlive her by a century.

"You've got it the wrong way," one of the mourners said.
They turned the coffin. A difficult manoeuvre.
Like a giant insect with no control over its feet.
But it fitted with less than an inch to spare.

Maybe that's the kind of funeral you get
For joking on the way to others' funerals.
For not crying. For being the clown.
Thinking life is unreasonable.
Beyond mourning. For considering
A car trip
Regardless of the destination
A car trip.

A Poem

I won't tell you the original,
The way Mr. Tatu Tanski told it to me
In his van on the way from Vaasa to Punkalaidun.

I changed some details
And added the bald hitchhiker called Auguste Dupin
So you would think it's a poem, not a joke.
Jokes are not appropriate, the world being what it is.
So here is the Poem:

A truck driver picked up a bald hitchhiker by the name Auguste Dupin.
The two men sat in the cabin talking this and that,
About the rain and receding hairlines.
Suddenly something moved behind them.
From the sleeping space behind the seats appeared
A small monkey in a red dress.
Why the monkey? Dupin asked, surprised.
The driver smiled,
Let me show you.

He slapped the monkey on the head.
Right away it jumped on the dashboard.
Started a strange striptease act,
Its brown eyes fixed on the driver all the time.

When it was over
The monkey put the dress back on and sat on the dashboard.
Fantastic, Dupin said.
Want to try? the driver asked.
I'd love to, Dupin replied,

Bowing his bald head toward the driver.
But please don't slap so hard.

On the way to Punkalaidun we stopped at a gas station for a coffee.
Are you crying? the lady asked.

A Song

Certain infra-sounds make us see ghosts.
It's not a matter of 'do you believe?'
They can put you in a room
Start the sound
And you will be scared, feel a chill
And see ghosts.

These sounds occur
Also spontaneously in nature.
A thunderstorm might tear off a roof.
But it can also
With exactly the right wind-speed
And with you in exactly the right spot in the room
Make you see dead people
The faces of whom
Are maybe up to you.

The rest is
Just particles in motion
Neutral but suddenly
Singing.

Idio(t)s

As kids we found a medical dictionary on my friend's parents' bookshelf
From the 1930's. I think. We flipped through
And there was a picture of a smiling man
With a funny moustache, sniffing a flower.
The caption read:
Idiot.

It became a classic for us.
Later I found a book in which
A 15th century Franciscan monk called Jesus' disciples
The twelue ydiotes.
Hilarious.
But actually it just means:
thei not lerned were.

In Ancient Greece one could find.
Not just philosophers but idiots.
A lot of them.
Idios (Gr.).
Meaning a private person,
Someone who doesn't have a say in public matters.
Most of us then.
Idiots. People not abreast,
People finding Jupiter and epigenetics
Quite insignificant. People smiling.
Somewhere on a field or a bus
Despite their age or lack of a limb.
Breathing with ease.
Sniffing an occasional flower.
Breathing dust or smoke or frost.

Looking at the stars
Now and millennia ago.
Humbled sincere.
By their own idiocy.
Asking
Which one you think is him or her or a god.

Carita Nyström

'My relation to poetry goes way back. At nine years old I had to spend a couple of weeks in hospital. As if to give me a break from boredom poems 'came to me' with crazy rhymes, rather nonsensical, but great fun.

A few years later I loved to read the classical poems in my father's anthology *All världens lyrik*. They were from the entire world, often with the original and the translation side by side. At that time I also kept a diary with poems of my own inserted. All without any intention to show anyone, this was my secret vice. Later my literary studies fostered even more self-criticism. So I was 35 when in 1975 I finally published poems. I have to admit that working with this project has reminded me of these earlier pleasant experiences.'

— Vaasa/Vasa, March 2018

The Greenhouse in Winter

It's January and behind the frosty glass
microscopic life survives under icy soil.

Suddenly green lines appear, next to
luscious red tomatoes, juicy cucumbers.

A secret connection prevails between
the greenhouse and my writing desk.

A Travelling Companion

I sit in the garden reading Jenni Diski –
Strangers on a Train.

Suddenly a dragonfly lands on my hand
and it lingers. I watch its eyes rotate.

I speak to it softly – it doesn't fly away.
In fact it travels with us.

The Wolf's Loop

In winter's blue hour children play.
They tread a circle in the snow, a cross inside it.

They run and chase each other laughing.
The game is ancient, possibly a rite.

Dark forest surrounds the scene, further away
you see gleaming eyes, teeth and claws?

Is it a wolf or a bear? Can the rite protect us?
People believed so long ago, trusted the magic.

The children keep running with happy shouts
and the suncross glimmers in the dark.

White Whales in the White Sea

The Queen of the Sea once reigned over these waters,
providing food and protection for coastal people.
But she tired of their greed and settled
for good deep down in the abyss.
Nine months of the year she covers
The White Sea with ice, from Kandalaksa
to Archangelsk.

A morning in July we board a ship
to take us to the Solovetskij Islands,
once the Gulag Archipelago.
Where are the white whales,
children of the Queen? Up on deck
we keep watch. Over there? No.
But suddenly a shoal appears,
and we watch them dance, their white backs
shimmer, undulating like waves.

Hilly islands float past. The boat is crowded,
priests, monks, pilgrims and tourists.
Our guide tells about a dolphinarium out there,
the only one in the world with white whales,
she invites us to attend for three hundred roubles.
And we will watch the whales, caught and tamed,
jumping for fish through hoops. We will hear
their song, and buy their paintings.
We will applaud.

Solovetskij

A wall, six metres wide, surrounds the kremlin.
The entrance is arched and old women kneel
crossing themselves before entering.
Meadows around the monastery are covered in
sweet-smelling clover. Soon bells are ringing.

Once this was Russia's richest monastery
and wealthy nobility made their pilgrimage here,
seeking blessings and forgiveness for their sins.
Monks in black cassocks hurry by
leaving their garden chores for prayers.

The first gulag was founded by Lenin
and perfected by Stalin. But even the tsars
found these islands suitable as prisons.
In the monastery there was torture,
prisoners dying of hard labour or starvation.

Can we really understand?
In the meadow the harebells nod:
Yes, it really was like that.

Lethe's River

One water for oblivion
one for remembrance.
I mix them and they flow together
running into Lethe's river.

Sand looks like waves,
undulating crests where
fair Unda Marina can dance.
In her footprints the light plays.

I write words in water,
poems and sinking songs.
A foot tramples the crests of sand,
glides into the water and –
                    is gone.

Loss

The floorboard squeaks
but no-one stands
in the doorway as before
        – you're gone

Everything around
is here – except you
At noon I walk alone
towards the forest

The barn stands where it
always has, and the road
turns in its usual way,
by the side stones lie

Approaching the forest
tears fill my eyes
I turn and
walk home

The Chaffinch in the Graveyard

How long I've waited for you, tiny finch.
Last year you arrived too soon, sliding
on the slippery snow, confused by cold.

This year I've waited, numb with grief,
till suddenly your voice
lifts my spirit in the endless grey.

On a branch in a sunlit lime-tree
you sing, drunk with life,
over rows of graves.

Give Grief Your Time

Give grief your time
give it space,
let it just be

At times it's like a child
weeping, longing for your
embrace and nearness

At times a dark mother
nearly choking you,
or a strict father with demands

At times a friend who listens
and senses your weakness,
strokes your hand kindly

A strange flower by the roadside
can it be, or just
a bird's feather
landing at your feet

Ge din tid åt sorgen

Ge din tid åt sorgen
låt den ta plats
låt den bara vara.

Ibland är den ett litet barn
som gråter, vill bli taget i famn,
känna din närhet.

Ibland en mörk och mäktig moder
som nästan kväver dig,
ibland en fader sträng som kräver

Ibland en vän som lyssnar.
En blick som ser din ömklighet,
en hand som smeker tröst.

En säregen blomma vid vägen
kan den vara, eller
ett fågelfjun som landat vid din fot.

Orrmoan – The Devil's Field

Dry moss, withered heather and crowberry
crack under my feet when I walk the devil's field

Here we used to walk, treading cautiously
on the mossy stones. Now it all seems new to me

The sun warms comforting when the memories
well forth. High above young fir-trees are singing –
\
                                               new songs

In The Archipelago

Wind and waves all over.
Clouds fly and the waves
turn the world inside out –

Water links the labyrinth of islands.
Waves flow and wash the shore.
Times float and islands rise.

Did Icarus fly here,
Lifted out of the labyrinth?
Is this where he fell?

The Labyrinth

Windings of stone covered
with lichen: grey, black and red –
A stone labyrinth surrounded by
four cairns, one for each cardinal point

Four sea-eagles – spirits of men lost at sea –
hover over the water, play in free air
And over there – a king's eagle rises
freed from earth's embrace

I rest for a while on one cairn,
inhale deep breaths of sea
My grief soars like an eagle
over ancient rocks

Moment

Watching stars light up the early evening,
I come to think they've always been there,
that only darkness makes them visible,
opening channels for them.

Enjoying violet clouds against a lime-coloured evening sky,
I realise that colours don't exist
I open the infinite images of my brain. Enter one of them

for a while. Then I return to the room and the objects in it:
the ticking clock, the table with a stack of books,
the black sea-shell from Isla Negra.